David Bowen's

# ENGLISH IDIOM

# SAY BOO TO A GOOSE

## SAY BOO TO A GOOSE!  -  The Human Psyche

### Exploring he English Idiom – Part Four

## Introduction

It happens repeatedly, we do it almost without thinking , make our observations about human behaviour in terms of the other world – that of beasts and birds, fish and annoying insects. A particularly fierce woman, and she's a tigress, a clumsy man a bull in a china shop.  Work hard, keep at it, and you're an eager beaver; become important and you're a big fish.

Will it ever stop?    I hope not, even although there are times for being formal and speaking 'proper English'. Does the Queen succumb?  Probably, yes.  Who in their senses would wish to banish 'cats' whiskers' or 'dogs' dinners'?  The language suffers if it is to be always stiff and correct as, indeed, does the 'terribly proper' human.

Which reminds me.  In the west of England 'proper job' means fine, everything going well, but you won't get that in London, Manchester, Glasgow or Belfast.

Here, in Book 4 of this series on English idiom, the message is 'loud and clear', as we say.  Human behaviour  and that of the 'lower' world' can be so alike that one may wonder where the one begins and the other ends.  Allow the goose to scare you and not say 'boo' to it and his friends  will get to know and you won't be in control of anything at all.

David Bowen

# CONTENTS

**Page**

# 1) ZOO LOGIC

Animal crackers in my soup,
Monkeys and rabbits loop the loop,
Gosh, oh my, oh gee what fun
Swallowing animals one by one.

Shirley Temple's song

ANIMAL  CRACKERS
in
her 1930'S Film

## 1.1) A Day with the Birds

### Birds generally

A bird (*dolly bird*)
>   attractive young lady

A bird in the hand is worth two in the bush (*saying*)
>   so be content with what is on offer

A little bird told me
>   someone told me, I forget who it was

Crestfallen (*drooping head*)
>   dispirited

Birds of a feather flock together *(saying)*
>   people go together according to their characteristics

dead as the dodo
>   obsolete – the dodo, now extinct, once a flightless
>   bird native to Mauritius

Do bird
>   serve a prison sentence

Early bird
>   early to rise from one's bed

Feather one's nest
>   accumulate ill-gotten riches

Get the bird
>   get into trouble

Jail-bird
>person sent to prison

Keep your pecker up
>hold your head up, stay cheerful and confident

Kill two birds with one stone (*or variant*)
>achieve two objectives from a single effort

(be) knocked down with a feather
>taken by surprise

Little children, like birds in their nests, should agree *(saying)*

Pecking order
>whether creature or person, each must take his natural place

Spread one's wings
>take on further commitments

Strictly for the birds
>not to be taken seriously

The bird has flown
>the quarry has escaped

The birds and the bees
>sex education

## Different birds

Canary
> informer to the police *(sings)*

## Crow

As the crow flies
> supposedly by the shortest route

Crow's feet
> wrinkles under the eyes

Crow's nest
> small observation platform near the top of a mast

Draw the crow (or *draw the short stra*w)
> come off worst in a situation

Pluck a crow with someone (or *a bone to pick*)
> have a complaint to make

Old crow
> unpleasant old lady

To crow over someone
> exult over another's ill luck

Stone the crows!
> exclamation of surprise

## Chicken

Chicken and egg situation
       puzzle over which came first

Chickenfeed (or a chicken)
       a trifling amount

Chicken-hearted
       timid, afraid

Chickens coming home to roost
       sins that find one out

Cock-a-hoop
       very pleased with oneself

Cock and bull
       nonsense

Cock of the walk
       conceited, boasting person

Don't count your chickens before they are hatched be sure of your
       gain before you speak of it

Fed like fighting cocks
       given the best food and conditions

Hen party
       female gathering – women only

Hen-pecked
       when a man is scolded by his wife or partner

**Cuckoo**

Cloud-cuckoo-land
　　fantasy dream-place

Cuckoo (*go cuckoo - don't be a cuckoo!*)
　　crazy person

Cuckoo-spit
　　frothy spit of insect on a plant to protect its larvae


**Dove**

Dove
　　peaceful person (*'lovey-dovey' addressing a child*)

Make a flutter in the dovecot (make feathers fly)
　　cause a disturbance


**Duck**

Bombay duck
　　no duck but Indian name for a local fish

Duckie
　　name when addressing a child

Lame duck
　　disadvantaged person

Like a duck to water
　　easily, without even thinking

Play ducks and drakes with
 squander

Sitting duck
 whoever makes an easy target

Ugly duckling
 someone despised by his own kind

Water off a duck's back
 no problem

## Eagle

Eagle eye
 far-sighted

## Gannet

Gannet
 greedy, like the sea-bird

## Goose

Cook someone's goose
 destroy another person's advantage

Goose-pimples
 small pimples on the human skin caused by cold or fear

Goose-step
 human marching with stiff knees and flat feet

Goosey
    stupid

Kill the goose that lays the golden egg
    spend the source of profit

Sauce for the goose, sauce for the gander *(saying)*
    the female should not be treated differently

Wild goose chase
    useless rushing about

Wouldn't say boo to a goose
    totally ineffective person


## Gull

Gull someone
    cheat, deceive


## Hawk

Hawkish
    greedy, opportunistic

Tell a hawk from a handsaw (*heronshaw, small heron*)
    have a practical knowledge of things, know what's what

Watch like a hawk
    keep a keen eye

Jay-walker
    careless walker, not looking out

## Magpie

Magpie
> person with a zeal for collecting things

## Owl

Night owl
> human who works or stays up at night

Not give a hoot
> not care about something

Owlish
> spectacled and blinking

## Ostrich

Ostrich-like
> 'dig one's head in the sand' to avoid seeing trouble

## Pigeon

Not my pigeon
> not my affair

Pigeon-hearted
> nervous, timid

Pigeon-hole
> small open storage compartment

Pluck a pigeon
>cheat a gullible person of his money

Stool-pigeon
>informer

Popinjay (*old name for pigeon*)
>conceited person

Rook someone
>steal

**Parrot**

Parrot-like
>repetition

Sick as a parrot
>very ill

v

**Peacock**

Proud as a peacock,
>showing off

Round robin
>petition with names arranged in a circle so as not to
>identify the originator(s)

## Skylark

Skylark around
>    play silly ticks

Up with the lark
>    rise early in the day

## Swallow

One swallow doesn't make a summer *(saying)*
>    Don't be too hasty with your judgement

## Swan

Swan about (or *around*)
>    be on show in somewhat aimless fashion

Swan off
>    wander off

Swan song
>    the final work of a musician or writer

## Vulture

Culture-vulture
>    person wholly devoted to the arts

## Wren

Wren
>    member of the former Women's Royal Naval Service

## 1.2)  Creatures of Home, Farm, Zoo, Mountain, Sea and Shore

**Ass**

Ass
>    silly ass, stupid person

Ass in a lion's skin
>    coward pretending to be brave

**Badger**

Badger a person
>    pester, harass

**Bat**

Bat around (U.S.)
>    wander around

Bats in the belfry
>    crazy in the head

Batty
		crazy

Blind as a bat
		completely blind

Like a bat out of hell
		very fast

Old bat
		unpleasant old woman

*with reference to the cricket bat*

Bat oneself in
		adjust to new surroundings

Never bat (flutter) an eyelid
		show no obvious concern

Off one's own bat
		impromptu, individual

Play with a straight bat
		make a straightforward approach

Right off the bat (U.S..
		immediately

## Bear

Bear
		rough, ill-mannered male person

Bear garden
> disorderly, turbulent assembly

Bear hug
> tight embrace with both arms clasped around the upper part of the body

Bear market
> falling values

Bear with a sore head
> irritable person

Bug-bear
> cause of irritation

Teddy bear
> child's cuddly plaything, named after 'Teddy' Roosevelt, U.S. President 1901-09, who was fond of bear-hunting

The Bear
> Russia

## Beaver

Beaver away
> keep working

Eager beaver
> zealous person

## Bull

Bull
>(military) what is considered by lower ranks to be unnecessary paperwork and instruction

Bull at a gate
>rash, hasty person

Bull-headed
>pushful, arrogant

Bull in a china shop
>clumsy individual

Bull-necked
>stiff-necked, obstinate, haughty

Bull's-eye
>centre of a target

(cock and) bull
>nonsense

Horns of a dilemma
>the bull will toss you, no matter what you do

Red rag to a bull
>whatever the cause of instant human anger

Take the bull by the horns
>make an immediate start on the job

## Calf

Kill the fatted calf
>plan a feast in someone's honour


## Camel

Camelish
>obstinate

Get the hump
>sulk, get angry

## Cat

A cat may look at a king *(saying)*
>he is no one's inferior

Care killed the cat *(*worry killed the cat) s*aying,*
>worry may also kill a human

Cat
>spiteful, malicious woman

Cat and dog  (fight like cat and dog*)*
>the ultimate troublesome relationship

Cat and mouse
>play with one's quarry

Cat burglar
>one who climbs to make his entry

Cat call
>cry of disapproval

Cat nap
> short rest

Cat's cradle
> a children's game

Cats' eyes
> reflectors on road surfaces

Cat's paw
> person used by another

Cat's pyjamas (or whiskers)
> something excellent

Catty
> spiteful

Enough to make a cat laugh
> supremely ridiculous

Fat cat
> overpaid , greedy person

Fur flying
> serious argument

Grin like a Cheshire cat
> make a wide grin

(have) Kittens
> be totally taken aback by something

Let the cat out of the bag
> reveal a secret

Like a cat on hot bricks
>jumpy, agitated

Like something the cat brought in
>something unpleasant

Moggy
>the common cat

No room to swing a cat
>very little space (*the cat here is a whip*)

Not a cat in hell's chance
>no chance at all

Old cat
>spiteful elderly female person

Pussyfoot
>excessive caution

Rain cats and dogs
>heavy rainstorm

See which way the cat jumps
>wait to see what happens

Set the cat among the pigeons
>cause a disturbance

Sourpuss
>bad-tempered person

Turn cat-in-pan
>change sides (*derived from the original French*)

Whip the cat
> make small economies

A cat has nine lives *(saying)*
> crossing a road could be one


## Cow *See also 'Calf')*

Cow
> *derogatory for* unpleasant woman
> *humorous:* all behind like the cow's tail (when
> > complaining of being behind with one's work)

Cowboy
> inefficient itinerant worker who demands large amounts of
> money for poor quality house repairs

Golden calf
> riches

Sacred cow
> venerable custom

Until the cows come home
> not for a very long time


## Crocodile

Crocodile
> moving queue of people

Crocodile tears
> false tears if of a human

## Deer

Deerstalker
> sportsman's helmet-shaped hat

## Dog

Bark's worse than his bite
> some fierce-looking men are said to be thus

Bitchy
> spiteful

Black dog
> depression

Dirty dog
> devious, untrustworthy person

Dog and boned
> stoned *(drunk) from Cockney rhyming slang*

Dog collar
> round white collar worn by a priest

Dog-eared
> pages bent back at the corner

Dog eat dog
> ruthless competition

Dog-end
> cigarette end

Dog-fight
> aerial combat

Dogged (dogged as does)
> persistent steady purpose

Doggone (U.S.)
> irritating, nuisance-making

Doggy-bag
> bag for left-overs at a restaurant

Dog house  *( oh dear, I'm in the dog-house!)*
> mythical place of correction for some domestic offence

Dog-in-the-manger
> wishing to deny others what one cannot have oneself

Dog-leg
> sharp bend

Dog paddle
> simple swimming stroke

Dog rose
> wild rose

Dog-rough
> rough, even for a dog

Dog's-body
> human drudge, one who is imposed upon

Dog-s breakfast, or dinner
> a nasty mess, or perhaps an over-dressed person

Dog's chance
>very little chance at all

Dogs of war
>havoc;  mercenary activity

Dog-tag
>soldier's identity disc

Dog-tired
>exhausted

Gay dog
>romancer

Give a dog a bad name and hang him
>a person whose reputation is questioned is said to be as
>good as convicted

Go dog (*Australia*)
>leave one's home to travel in the wilds

Go to the dogs
>deteriorate rapidly

Hair of the dog
>a little more of what caused the trouble

Hang dog
>gloomy, sad

Help a lame dog over a stile
>give aid to someone in distress

Lead the life of a dog
>reckoned to be a poor one for the majority

Let sleeping dogs lie
> do not stir up trouble

Lie doggo
> stay quiet, hidden away

Like a dog with two tails
> jubilant

Mucky pup *(puppy)*
> child in a mess, spilled something

Old dog
> old man, experienced sailor

Put on the dog
> pretentious attitude

See a man about a dog
> visit the toilet (comfort room)

Shaggy dog story
> one that has little point and goes on and on

Shouldn't happen to a dog
> totally disgraceful situation

Tail wags the dog
> what is important takes control`

Throw to the dogs
> abandon what is still useful

Top dog
> experienced or important person

Underdog
> inferior position

Watchdog
> well paid official appointed to oversee fair dealing

Yap
> speak constantly and noisily

## *Sayings*

Every dog has his day
> even an unfortunate person must get his chance sometimes

You can't teach an old dog new tricks
> the older one gets, the more difficult it is to absorb new ways of doing things

No point keeping a dog if you have to bark yourself
> doing the work entrusted to your servant

## **Donkey**

Donkey
> stupid person

Donkey-work
> drudgery

Donkey's years
> a long period of time

Talk the hind legs off a donkey
> keep talking

## Dragon

Dragon
> any human being considered as fierce of
> character as the mythical monster

Dragons' teeth (military)
> upright obstacles on the ground

Sow dragons' teeth
> stir up trouble


## Elephant

(an) elephant in the room
> a person to be ignored

Bathe the elephants
> child's mistake for 'brave the elements'

(let an) elephant pass while straining at a gnat
> allow larger transgressions to pass with impunity while
> taking care to avoid minor ones

Elephants' ears
> leaves of certain plants

Pink elephants
> hallucinations

See the elephant (*U.S.*)
> see all there is to see

White elephant
> object that is more trouble than it's worth

## Fox

Fox (*U.S.*)
>    attractive young woman

Foxy
>    sly, cunning person

Foxed
>    brown marks on paper caused by mildew

Foxhole
>    small depression in the ground used by the
>    military for cover

Old fox
>    cunning old man *(said, perhaps, with a knowing smile)*


## Goat

Get someone's goat
>    irritate

Goat *('silly billy', 'billy-goat')*
>    foolish person

Play the giddy goat
>    fool around

Scapegoat
>    whoever takes the blame for others' mistakes

Separate the sheep from the goats
>    divide the worthy from the unworthy

**Hare**

Hare along
    go very fast


**Hog (*see also, pig* )**

Bring one's hogs to market
    make a mess of something

Drive one's hogs to market
    snore loudly

Eat high off the hog
    take more than one's fair share

Go the whole hog
    do something completely, thoroughly

Hog it (hoggish)
    eat greedily

Hog the limelight
    seek all the praise

Hog's back
    hill ridge; the hull of a ship

Hogwash
    nonsense

Hog wild ( *U.S.A.)*
    go berserk

## Horse

Back the wrong horse
    make an error of judgement

(don't) change horses in mid-stream
    avoid dangerous manoeuvres

Colt's tooth
    youthful pleasures

Dark horse
    person whose plans and capabilities are unknown

Flog a dead horse
    continue with a subject that is considered closed

From the horse's mouth *(or 'straight from the horse's mouth')*
    direct, authentic

(don't look a) gift-horse in the mouth
    accept a gift gracefully

Give a horse his head
    allow him to go as fast as he likes

High horse
    arrogant attitude

Hobby horse
    favourite topic or personal pursuit

Hold your horses
    wait! - don't go yet

Horse-and-buggy (*U.S.*)
  old-fashioned

Horse around
  fool about

Horse bargaining
  hard bargaining

Horse laugh
  loud boisterous laugh

Horse-neck
  ginger ale with spirit

Horse of a different colour
  a different matter altogether

Horse play
  rough play between the sexes with sexual motif

Horse sense
  plain common sense

Horses for courses
  people perform best within their natural
  environment

Horse trading
  hard bargaining

Let something ride
  leave alone, take noaction

Mare's nest
  what turns out to be imaginary

'The mare's the better horse' *(saying)*
>  the wife is the better partner

Mares' tails
>  streaks of high *cirrostratus* cloud that presage rain,
>  also known as  *hens' scarts*

Nag
>  home-bred horse

(a) nod's as good as a wink to a blind horse
>  useless to make a hint if the other cannot see it

'No good shutting the stable door after the horse has bolted'
>  *(saying)*

One-horse race
>  no real competition

One-horse town (*mainly U.S.)*
>  one with few amenities

Put the cart before the horse
>  reverse the natural procedure, get things in the wrong
>  order

Ride down
>  overtake, trample

Ride for a fall
>  ruthless behaviour

Ride one's high horse
>  put on grand and superior airs

Ride out
>come safely through a storm or other hazard

Take for a ride
>dupe, deceive

Trojan horse
>concealment

White horse
>white-topped wave , figure of a horse sculptured into a chalk down, rescuer in a financial bid

Wild horses wouldn't drag me
>refuse utterly to go along with some plan

Willing horse
>obliging worker

Work-horse
>ever busy person or machine

*'You can take a horse to water but you cannot make him drink'*
>human power is limited

Hound
>contemptible person

## Hyena

Laugh like a hyena
>laugh with a piercing shriek

## Kangaroo

Kangaroo court
> illegal court controlled by a mob


## Lamb (*See also 'Sheep'*)

Be a lamb and...'
> a request made to a young child

Ewe lamb
> dearest person

In two shakes of a lamb's tail
> very quickly, immediately

'Lambs' ears
> hazel catkins

'Lambs' wool ' clouds
> small *cumulus* clouds of fine weather

Like a lamb to the slaughter,
> innocently

Mutton dressed as lamb
> older woman dressing in the younger style

Poor lamb
> sympathy for an unfortunate child

'There's a lamb'
> assumption that a child so addressed will conform

## Leopard

A leopard cannot change his spots
      personal traits are not reversible


## Lion

Lion
      human member of an international organisation

Lion-heart (*lion-hearted*)
      courageous person

Lionise
      treat as a celebrity

Lion's mouth
      wherever it's a dangerous place to be

Lion's share
      the greater part

Twist the lion's tail
      annoy Great Britain


## Lynx

Lynx-eyed
      keen-sighted

## Monkey

Cheeky monkey
    cheeky person

Get one's monkey up
    get angry

Have a monkey on one's back
    addicted to drugs

Make a monkey of
    make a fool of

Monkey (*monkey about*)
    practical joking,  playing tricks

Monkey business
    mischief

Monkey fallen from one's tree
    one's purpose in ruins, frustrated

Monkeying about
    pranks, foolery

Monkey jacket
    close fitting naval, or other, jacket

Monkey on one's back
    humiliated

Monkey puzzle
    type of coniferous tree

Monkey-shine (*U.S.*) & monkey-tricks
>    foolery

Not give a monkey's
>    not care

Wild man of the woods
>    orang-utan

## Mule

Kick like a mule
>    a hard, sharp kick

Muleish
>    stubborn

## Ox

Black ox
>    depression

Ox-bow
>    horse-shoe bend (u-shaped)

Ox-eye
>    storm cloud sufficiently distant as to appear as a
>    white eye or hand on the horizon

Strong as an ox
>    very strong indeed

## Pig

Guinea pig
   be the object of an experiment

Make a pig of oneself
   eat greedily or excessively

Make a pig's ear of something
   make a mess of it

Pig-headed
   ignorant

Pig in a poke
   Something bought without knowing its valu

Pig in clover
   moneyed person with coarse behaviour

Pig it
   live or stay in squalid surroundings

Piggy-bank
   child's money box shaped like a pig, usually of china

Piggy in the middle
   awkwardly placed person, between rivals

Pig out
   eat like gluttons, go on a binge

Pigs might fly
   it will never happen

Pig-sty
> any dirty place

You cannot make a silk purse out of a sow's ear *(saying)*
> You cannot make something good from material of
> inferior quality


## Pony

Pony *(in terms of money)*
> twenty-five U.K. pounds

Shanks' pony
> need for a human to rely on his own two feet


## Possom (small furry quadruped native to *Australia*)

Play possom
> Disguise one's intentions

Stir the possum *(Australia)*
> even things up


## Rabbit

Bunny-rabbit
> child's name for a rabbit

Bunny-girl
> scantily dressed girl with a fluffy tail at a nightclub

Pull rabbits out of a hat
> conjurer's trick

Rabbit on or away
> talk incessantly

Shark
> unscrupulous individual who exploits and cheats

## Sheep (*See also 'Lamb'*)

Be killed for a sheep as a lamb
> take the greater risk if the punishment is the same

Black sheep
> person considered to be the reprehensible member of a family

Bleat like a sheep
> complain, talk a lot of nonsense

Make sheep's eyes
> make wistful eyes to attract a member of the opposite sex

Separate the sheep from the goats
> identify the superior members of any group

Sheepish
> bashful, shy

Sheep's head
> 'all jaw' – compulsive talker

**Sloth**

Slothful
>    lazy *(hardly a fair comparison seeing that the sloth is slow 'by design')*

**Snake**

Snake in the grass
>    treacherous person

Viper in one's bosom
>    one who will betray

**Stag**

Stag party
>    all-male alcoholic celebration, especially for a bridegroom on he night before his wedding

**Tiger**

Hold a tiger by the tail
>    one step from disaster

Paper tiger
>    more of a theoretical than a real one

Tiger/tigress
>    fierce, formidable man or woman

## Turtle

Turn turtle
    turn on one's back, capsize

## Whale

Whale of a time
    an exciting, highly enjoyable, time

## Wolf

Cry wolf!
    give a false alarm

Keep the wolf from the door
    have sufficient to eat

Lone wolf
    whoever likes to go it alone

See a wolf
    be tongue-tied

Throw to the wolves
    abandon

Wolf in sheep's clothing
    pretence of friendship

Wolfish
    rapacious

Wolf it
>> eat greedily

Wolf whistle
>> crude whistle of admiration from man to woman

## Zebra

Zebra  (crossing)
>> striped street crossing where pedestrians have
>> precedence over vehicles

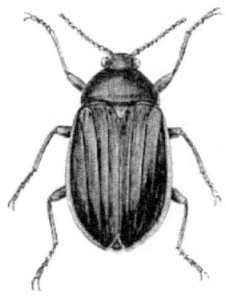

## 1.3) Among smaller creatures and manifestations

**Beetle**

Beetle brows
    jutting eyebrows

Beetle off
    start moving and go somewhere

Ferret
    searching out a secret

**Frog**

Frog in the throat
    hoarseness of a human

Frog-march
    march a person with his hands tied behind his back

Leap-frog
    jump over a person's back that is bent horizontally

## Hare

First catch your hare
>ensure you have what you need before you decide
what to do with it

Hare-brained
>crazy idea

Raise a hare
>introduce a spurious line of argument in order
to deflect attention

Run with the hare and hunt with the hounds
>play a double game

## Lizard

Lounge lizard
>lazy, useless person who 'sticks around' the place

## Mole

Mole
>spy

Make a mountain out of a mole-hill
>make an unnecessary fuss

## Mouse

Mouse
> dull, colourless person

Mouse about
> search for something, prowl around

Mouse on the table
> a problem too big to be ignored

'Mouse-trap'
> indifferent cheese

Mousey
> nondescript grey colour or complexion

Poor as a church mouse
> poor, because there is normally little food to be
> found in a church

The best-laid plans of mice and men
> a warning that neither can be guaranteed

Today the man, tomorrow the mouse
> fortune can be fickle

When the cat's away the mice will play *(saying)*


Oyster
> human desires contained within a single shell

## Rat

Rat (rat-bag, *U.S.)*
> despicable person

Like a drowned rat
> soaked to the skin, dishevelled

Rat on
> inform

Rat pack
> crowd of rowdies, or worse

Rat race
> fiercely competitive struggle

Rat run
> minor road heavily used by traffic

Ratty
> angry, bad-tempered

Smell a rat
> have suspicions

Shrew
> bad-tempered, scolding woman

Shrimp
> a small, slightly-built person

Skunk
> odious, highly contemptible person

**Slug**

Slug (sluggish)
    unwilling to do very much

**Snail**

Snail (snail's pace)
    painfully slow movement

**Toad**

Toad (toady)
    fawning on a person

Toad-in-the-hole
    batter  with sausage or other meat filling

**Weasel**

Weasel-faced
    sharp, pointed face

Weasel words
    ones that are intentionally ambiguous or misleading

Weasel out
    avoid an obligation

## Worm

Worm
> lowest form of creature on earth

Can of worms
> difficult and complex situation

(the) worm may turn
> even a weak person my get the chance to retaliate

Worm one's way in
> ingratiate oneself

Worm out of a person
> extract information little by little

Even the worm will turn *(saying)*
> the weakest will retaliate if pushed too far

## 1.4) Very small creatures

**Bee**

Bee's knees,
    something absolutely excellent

Bee in one's bonnet
    an obsession

**Bug**

Bug
    A variety of meanings, from micro-organisms to hidden
    microphones

Bug-bear
    object of annoyance or possibly baseless fear

## Butterfly

Butterfly
>a flighty person who, like a butterfly, flits about
>from one place to another

Butterflies in the stomach
>fluttering, nervous

Butterfly bush
>buddleia

Butterfly kiss
>one with fluttering eyelashes

## Flea

Flea in one's ear
>get angry

Fleamarket
>place for sale of second-hand clothing and other goods

## Fly

Fly in the ointment
>problem, disadvantage

Fly on the wall
>imaginary personal access to conversations that one might
>like to hear

No flies on a person
>one who is familiar with the world around him

## Gnat

(straining at a) gnat while letting an elephant pass
        avoiding minor transgressions while making
        larger ones with impunity


## Grasshopper

Grasshopper
        copper (policeman) in Cockney rhyming slang

Grasshopper mind
        unable to concentrate on any one thing

(merry as a )grig
        happy as a cricket (grasshopper), said to be that
        on account of its chirping


## Hornet

(stir up a) hornet's nest
        cause a whole lot  of trouble


## Moth

(put in) mothballs
        put temporarily out of use


## Spider

Blow away the cobwebs
        take a walk in the fresh air

Spidery
> thinly radiating spokes and thin, elongated characters as a style in handwriting

Spiderwork
> lace stitching

Spiderman
> one who works on exposed tall buildings

## Wasp

Waspish
> overcritical person with little good to say about others

Wasps' nest
> where one is confronted on all sides by enemies

Wasp-tongued
> biting tongue

Wasp waist
> that of a very slender person

## 2) THE HUMAN TOUCH

*Accentuate the positive,*
*Eliminate the negative ...*
*(from one of Bing Crosby's songs)*

## 2.1) A - C

### (1) Positive

Above suspicion,  honest
Apple of one's eye, highly valued person
Born with a silver spoon, cosseted, protected
Better half , one's husband, wife, or partner
Big noise, important person
Call a spade a spade, speak bluntly
Clean sweep, unhindered by the past
Clued up, well informed
Courage of one's convictions, fearless approach
Cut one's coat to suit, spend appropriately

## (2) Negative

Bag of tricks, deceitful person
Be all over you, flatterer
Be up to something, planning secretly
Big mouth, boastful person
Bite the dust, come to nothing
Bit of fluff or of all right (*derog*), attractive young lady
Bundle of nerves, jumpy, nervous
Burn the midnight oil, work or stay up late
Cheesed off, disappointed, bored
Chink in one's armour, open to attack
Chip on the shoulder, bear a grudge
(have had one's) chips, tried and failed
Cold as charity, impersonal nature

## (3) Neutral Ground

Alike as two peas in a pod, the same features
All and sundry, everyone
All things to all men, tries to please everyone
Also ran, the other competitors in a race
A mixed bag, varied group of people or objects
A stranger to something, no experience
Chip off the old block, like one's parent
Chop and change, adjusting to conditions
Clip someone's wings, reduce the power of another

## 2.2) D - F

### (1) Positive

Don't know one is born, a problem-free life
Easy on the eye, pleasant to behold
(have the) edge on another, superior by competition
Good egg, worthy person
*Enfant terrible,* new ideas and inventions
(in a) fair way of something, successful
Feather in one's cap, achievement
(both) feet on the ground, well informed, ready
Fit as a fiddle, in good physical condition
Fighting fit, a well-trained body
Firing on all cylinders, working perfectly
(of the) first water, the best possible
Friend at court, influential person
Front runner, one who excels in his own activity

### (2) Negative

Daggers drawn, sworn enemies
Dead loss, considered useless
Death warmed up, very ill and frail
Diehard, sticking to one's original way of life
Done for, ruined
Don't give a fig, don't care
Down at heel, shabby and neglecting oneself

Down in the dumps, depressed
Down on his luck, suffering each day
Drip, stupid and inefficient
(bad) egg, worthless person
Make an exhibition of oneself, behave foolishly
Eye on the main chance, self-seeking
(on the) fiddle, dishonest
Fifth-columnist, traitor to one's country
Firebrand, out to cause trouble
(throw a) fit, give an angry response
Fly-by-night, one doesn't hear him go
Fools' paradise, unrealistic state of mind
(making) free with someone, taking advantage
Full of himself, smug, self satisfied

## (3) Neutral Ground

Dead ringer, spitting image
Dressed to kill (to the nines), intending to impress
Easy come, easy go, earn it and spend it
Fancy man *(derog),* someone's lover
Father or mother of, extreme example
Flesh and blood, relatives

**2.3) G - I**

### (1) Positive

Gentle sex, the female sex
Get a new lease of life, better all round
Get into one's stride, reach normal performance
Given moral support, encouragement
God's gift, highly thought-of person
Go from strength to strength, steady progress
Going strong, active and well-placed
Golden boy, talented young man
Good as gold, well-behaved child
Go through with, willing to persist
Go to any length, stop at nothing if worth-while
Grin and bear it, willing to endure unpleasant things
(take a grip on oneself, resist foolish temptations
(come to) grips with, be able to deal with problems
Grow on someone, become liked, popular
Happy as a sandboy, very happy
Have a good thing going, income, relationship
Have a strong stomach, not easily sickened
Head screwed on, sensible person
High-flier, successful, continually ambitious
Honourable mention, award

In for a penny, in for a pound, fully committed
In the saddle, in control

## (2) Negative
Gift of the gab, tediously talkative
Gold-digger, female exploiting a male person
Gone to nothing, physically wasted
Gone to pieces, out of one's mind
Good for nothing, hopeless individual
Go to seed, neglect health and appearance
(be) green, suffer from inexperience
Half-baked, stupid person
Hard-boiled, unfeeling and unemotional
Hard-liner, guaranteed to take strong action
Have a nerve, no respect or feeling for others
Heavy going, sombre, limited speech
High-falutin', grand manner, pretentious
Holy terror, much feared
In a cleft stick, unable to move
In a lather, in a worked-up state

## (3) Neutral Ground
Grey eminence, influential person in the background
(force of) habit, regular practice, difficult to change
In or out of someone's good or bad books, treated
        with favour or otherwise
In or out of step, with or without the same objective
In someone's wake, following closely

## 2.4) J - L

### (1) Positive

(hit the) jackpot, gain money or good position
Jetset, the rich on their world travel
Jolly along, be on good terms with whoever
Just the ticket, content, very pleased

Keen as mustard, very enthusiastic
Know one's own mind, reach own decisions
Knows his stuff, well-informed
Knows what's what, not easily deceived
Knows where he stands, realist

Leading light, expert in his field of knowledge
Level-headed, calm, good sense
Listens to reason, understanding personality
Live in style, luxuriously
Live something down, recover from an earlier mistake
Live wire, full of energy

**(2) Negative**
Jump the queue, push oneself forward

Ladies' man, excessive ly attentive to females
Latchkey child, returns daily to an empty house
Law unto himself, ignores orders he doesn't like
Lays down the law, expects all to obey
Leaves in the lurch, unfaithful partner
Lily-livered, cowardly
(the) limit, impossible to tolerate him or her
Lines his pocket, money doubtfully acquired
Lunatic fringe, crazy people

**(3) Neutral Ground**
Just desserts, as one is entitled, good or bad

Keeps his own counsel, mostly silent

(resting on one's) laurels, on past achievements
(in the) limelight, acclaim on stage or film
Live in an ivory tower, detached existence

## 2.5) M – O

### (1) Positive

Make a name for oneself, become well known
Make good, have a record of achievement
Make much of something, enthuse
Make something of oneself, progress
Make the best of a bad job, try hard
(in the) making, developing plan
(in the) manner born, privileged start
Man of the moment, exceptional person
Marked man, considered for promotion
Method in one's madness, there is a plan
Mind of one's own, independent response
(doesn't) miss a trick, alert, aware
Moral support, encouragement
More than one string to his bow, many talents
(clear someone's) name, prove his innocence
Nearest and dearest, one's family
Not a bad sort, decent average type
(think) nothing of it, it's my normal work
(be) nuts about, very enthusiastic
Old hand at something, done it for years
One in a million, exceptional person
(come into) one's own, show one's ability
One's own man, self-employed

(do) one's own thing, work as one wishes
(have) one's own way, take personal decisions
On the level, fair, honest
On the straight and narrow, a virtuous life
On to a good thing, excellent prospects
(go) overboard for something, very enthusiastic
Own up to, confess one's error


## (2) Negative

Mad as a hatter, crazy
Make a muck of something, spoil it
Mealy-mouthed, smooth, insincere
Money to burn, careless spender
More fool you, verbal admonishment
(too) much for someone, beyond his capability
Muck-rake, disclose unpleasant facts about another
Mug's game, only a fool would participate
(hard as) nails, unfeeling, unemotional
Name-dropper, claiming important friends
(your) name is mud, strong complaint
(call someone) names, insult a person
Narrow-minded, unwilling to compromise
Nasty piece of work, behave unacceptably
Nervy, jumping about, never still
No oil painting, ugly features
Not a patch on, inferior to another
Not a penny to his name, struggling existence
(come to) nothing, fail totally
(have) nothing to do with, make no contact
Not in the same street as, not to be compared
Not stand the sight of, feel antipathy to another
Not the word for it, hardly strong enough

(stick one's) oar in, interfere
(at) odds with, in disagreement

Over the odds, more than it should have been
(in a bad) odour, have a bad reputation
(all) off, cancelled
(badly)off, lacking in personal essentials
(go) off, deteriorate – especially food
On a sticky wicket, difficult circumstances
On a tight rein, under another's control
On the street, homeless
Out at the elbow, shabbily dressed
Out for something, one might be suspicious
Out of sorts, unwell
Overdo it, work too hard  or too long
(all) over one, paying excessive attention
(get one's) own back, exact revenge

### (3) Neutral Ground
Make a splash, attract attention
(not be able to) make it out, not understanding
(one's mate, partner
(burn the) midnight oil, work or sit up late
(in the same) mould, closely similar
Mum's the word, stay silent
No object, no objection (*distance no object!*)
Not for love nor money, on no account
*Nothing ventured, nothing gained, saying*
Not set the Thames on fire, unexceptional
Not stand on ceremony, no formalities
Not to stand it, not endure
Not up to much, mediocre
Oldie, elderly person
Old maid, unmarried lady of later age
Old-school, living by past standards
Old -timer, did the same job for years
(just) one of those things, unavoidable
One's own man, self-employed
On one's tod, alone

On the rebound, new love after failure
On the shelf *(derog))* long time unmarried
 On the spur of the moment, suddenly
On the tiles, away from home
On tick, on credit
Opposite number, does the same job elsewhere
Out of touch, out of communication
Out on a limb, working at a distance
Outsider, not within one's own group

## 2.6) P – R

### (1) Positive
(stay the) pace, maintain progress
(beg someone"s) pardon, apologise
(take in good) part, not be offended
Patience of Job, virtually limitless
Pay the piper, pay what you owe
(the) penny drops, one begins to understand
Pep talk, lecture to arouse enthusiasm
(give someone a) piece of one's mind, speak frankly
Pin one's hope on , rely on the favourable aspect

Play one's trump card, do something potent
Pleased as Punch, absolutely delighted
Plough back, invest the profits in the business
Practise what one preaches, avoid hypocrisy
Presence of mind, quick thinking when called for
(sitting pretty, in a favourable position
(someone's) pride and joy, highly esteemed
Pride oneself in something, do it well
Pull oneself together, take a hold of oneself
Pull one's weight, accept one's share of the work
Pull something off, succeed in doing something
Pull up one's socks, do something better
(to some) purpose, for a useful result
Push-over, easy job
Put in a good word, as support for another
Put on a pedestal, depict as a shining example
Put oneself in another's place, show understanding
Put up with, endure patiently

Quick on the uptake, immediate response
Quids in, in a favoured position
Quite something, very remarkable

Rally round, give needful assistance
Reckon on something, depend on it
Red-blooded, active, manly, virile
Redeeming feature, positive side to a fault
Red-letter day, one of pleasant surprises
(of) repute, well thought of
(strike it) rich, successful business
Right-hand man, trusted deputy
(keep on someone's) right side, stay on good terms
(a) roaring trade, successful business
Rolling in it, supposedly very rich
(know the) ropes, familiar with procedure
(a) run for one's money, something to show for it

## (2) Negative

(send someone) packing, dismiss a person
(beyond the) pale, unacceptable behaviour
(grease someone's palm, offer a bribe
Palm something off, pretend without defect
Paper over the cracks, pretend all is well
(below) par, below the standard, or unwell
Passed one's best, less active or efficient
Passed over, rejected in favour of another
(strike a bad) patch, encounter problems
(turn up like a bad) penny, be unwelcome
Perish the thought, hope it will never happen
(go to) pieces, have a nervous breakdown
Pinch and scrape, exist on very little
Pipe down! Keep quiet!
Play one person against another, intrigue
(line one's) pockets, obtain money dishonestly
(go to) pot, get progressively worse
Pot calling the kettle black, both the same
(hot) potato, currently troublesome situation
Practical joker, plays stupid jokes
(out of )practice, poor performance
(sharp) practice, unjust dealing
Pressed for something, short of time, money, etc
(a) prey to something, something not right
Price oneself out of the market, charge too much
Puffed out or up, conceited
Pull the wool (over someone's eyes), deceive
Punch-drunk, in a daze, confused
(give or get the) push, dismiss or be dismissed
Pushed for something (short of – same as 'pressed'
Put a spoke in someone's wheel, cause a hindrance
Put on an act (put it on), make a pretence
Put someone in the wrong, be the cause of it
Put someone off his stroke, cause him problems

Put-up job, create a false appearance
Put upon someone, make unreasonable demands

Queer someone's pitch, spoil another's plan(s)
(jump the) queue, take another's place in front
(cut to the) quick, hurt feelings

(go to) rack and ruin, be in a state of neglect
(lose one"s) rag, one's temper
(go off the) rails, crazy behaviour
Rake something up, what was better left unsaid
(on the) rampage, striking out
Ranting and raving, uncontrollable outburst
(take the)rap, the blame
Read the riot act, declare what is unacceptable
(take for a)  ride, trick, deceive
Riding for a fall, behave so as to cause disaster
 Riotous living, extravagant, disastrous
 (on the) rocks, marriage break or whisky on ice
(make a) rod for one's) back, cause oneself problems
Rub salt into the wound, increase the pain
Rub up the wrong way, irritate
(on the) run, escaping
Run out on, abandon
Run riot, uncontrolled
(take a) running jump! rude command
(in a) rut, cannot progress

## (3) Neutral Ground
(put something through its) paces, test it
Pack up, leave work
(be at) pains to point out, be sure to do so
(on) paper, in theory
(make a) pass, seek a romantic attachment
(hold one's) peace, stay silent
Pick and choose, choose carefully

Pin someone down, require to make a promise
Pin something on someone, prove responsibility
(at a) pinch, in an emergency
(know one's) place, accept one's role in society
Play a losing game, what might pay in the long run
(make a) play for something, try to obtain it
Play second fiddle, a secondary role
(the) plot thickens, deepens
Poles apart, very different from each other
(watched) pot never boils, wait longer when expecting
Press something into service, emergency use
Pressure  group, attempt to influence a decision
(bring) pressure to bear, force to do something
*Pride goes before a fall (saying)* excess of confidence
(keep a low)profile, stay unnoticed
Pull out all the stops, use maximum effort
Pull strings, use influence to assist a cause
Pull the strings, operate something
Put a spurt on, hurry
Put paid to, put an end to
Put someone off, decline or postpone an invitation
Put the tin lid on, finish completely
Put two and two together, realise the significance

(out of the) question, impossible, can't be done
(on the) qui vive, on the alert
Quits *(call it quits),* nothing owing either way

(at) random, without a particular plan
Rank and file, the majority of people
(close) ranks, act together in a defensive manner
Rarin to go, keen to make a start
(in the) raw, in its natural state
Read between the lines, assess the true meaning
(take something as) read, assume it to be correct
(for) real, genuine, true

(within) reason, in so far as it makes good sense
(off the (record), not made public or confirmed
Reel off something, recite quickly without pausing
Refresh one's memory, think back in detail
Resting on one's laurels, relying on one's past
(good) riddance, pleased to have it no longer
(in one's) right mind, acting rationally
Rough and ready, a working arrangement
(all-)rounder, able to act in different roles
Rub along with, a person's daily company
Runner-up, taking second place
Run riot, run out of control
Runs in the family, characteristics, good or bad
Run through something, take a quick look at it

## 2.7) S - U

### (1) Positive
Salt of the earth, worthy person
Show one's paces, what one can do
Sold on something, enthusiastic
(make) something of a person, develop his skill
Spoiling for something, eager

Spur someone on, encourage
Stand corrected, confess one's mistake
Stand fast, refuse to yield
Stand or fall by, committed to a single aim
Stand up for someone, make known your support
Steal the show, receive overwhelming acclaim
Step into dead men's shoes, inherit a position
Still going strong, remain active
Strike a balance, compromise
Strike the right note, meet with approval
Strong point, special quality
(one's) strong suit, in what one excels
Struck on a person or on something, approve greatly

Take someone up on something, accept an offer
Take in one's stride, cope easily
Take the liberty of doing, use initiative
Take up the cudgels on another's behalf, defend
Take up with someone, gtet friendly with
Thick as thieves, very friendly with another
Thrilled to bits, delighted
Tickled pink, highly amused
Tower of strength, timely support
Trial and error, learn by experience
Turn over a new leaf, reform one's character

## (2) Negative
Score off someone, cause him to look foolish
Shoot a line, boast of what may not be true
Short on, lacking something
(at) sixes and sevens, in disagreement
Slow on the uptake, slow to respond
Soft touch, one who is easily deceived
Speak with a forked tongue, tell lies
Stage fright, lack of confidence in a public role
Standoffish, unfriendly

Stand someone up, fail to keep a promise
Steer clear of, avoid
Step down, give up a position
Stew in one's own juice, be left with problems
Stick-in-the-mud, refuse to accept new ideas
Sticky fingers, stealing
Strike a bad patch, get into difficulty
(in the) soup, in trouble

Tell tales, disclose on another
Thick as two short planks, stupid person
Throw a spanner in the works, spoil a plan
Throw good money after bad, beyond rescue
Throw in the towel, give up the attempt
Throw one's weight around, dictatorial person
Throw up the sponge (*same as 'in the towel'*)
Tied up, too busy to tackle anything else
Tied up in knots, confused state of mind
Tight corner, difficult position
Tile loose, crazy person
(little) tin god, thinks a lot of himself
Torn between, a problem of alternatives
Touch someone for, to give or lend money
Tough customer, difficult to deal with
Tread on someone"s corns, interfere
Trick of the trade, perhaps dishonest dealing
Turn one off, feeling of dislike

Ugly as sin, very ugly
Unknown quantity, little known about a person
Upstage another, take his glory and his credit
Up the spout, ruined
Up to his usual tricks, behaving deceitfully
Up to something, likely to be plotting

## (3) Neutral Ground

Same old story, keeps happening
Search one's soul, examine one's conscience
See what I mean? It's just as I told you
Softly, softly, proceed with caution
Something up one's sleeve, not yet revealed
Sort something out, arrange for something
Speaks volumes, gives eloquent support
Spin it out, make it last a long time
Spring something on someone, sudden idea
Square up, settle obligations
Stage manage, take charge of the operation
Stamp something out, crush or subdue
Stand down, withdraw
Stand for, represent, tolerate
Stand in for, deputise
Standing by, awaiting call
Steady on, don't get worked up!
Stonewall, resist opponents' incursion

Tells its own tale, see it for yourself
There you are! I am right!
Thrash something out, discuss and decide
(give a) tinkle, make a telephone call
Tip the wink, let me know
Tit for tat, give as one gets, blow for blow
Tone down, soften
(argue the) toss, who will win, or what else
Toss-up, matter of speculation
Touch a chord, a memory
Touchy-feely, proceed cautiously
Try that for size, what do you think of it?
(to the) tune of, amounting to (approximately)
Turn-up for the books, unexpected

Under someones wing, given tutelage, protection
Ups and downs, periods of good and bad luck
Upshot, result
Upsides with someone, at the same level and status
Use one's loaf, one's brain
U-turn, reverse direction

## 2.8) V - Z

*Variety is the spice of life (saying)*

**(1) Positive**
(the) very thing, just what is needed

Walk on air, extremely happy
(have a) way with, good at managing
Well and good, quite acceptable
Well up on something, have all-round knowledge
Winning streak, run of good luck
Wish someone joy, hope all goes well
With a will, energetically
Work out, happen as planned, be successful
(give someone the)works, the full treatment
　　　*(at one time, this was a threat)*
Works a treat, works very well
(none the) worse for something, no resulting harm

## (2) Negative
Vicious circle, bad made worse by result

Walk all over someone, ignore rights and feelings
Walk out on, abandon
(back to the) wall, facing great difficulty
(drive up the) wall, make someone angry, confused
Want for something, be lacking something
(on the) warpath, in an angry mood
(been in the) wars, showing signs of injury
Washed out, totally lacking in energy
Whipping boy, punished for others' mistakes
Whistle for something, unlikely to get it
Whoop it up, noisy party
Window dressing, lacking in real value
(have one's) wires crossed, misunderstanding
Wise to, aware of dangers and problems
Witch-hunt, search and persecute
With one's tail between one's legs, ashamed
Without rhyme or reason, no explanation
With the best will in the world, not possible
(at one's) wit's end, totally confused
Woe betide, warning whoever will disregard
Woe to the person who ..., threat of vengeance
Wool-gatherer, absent-minded person
Work something off, take physical exercise
Worn out, severely fatigued
Worse for wear, tired, dishevelled appearance
(if) worst comes to worst, worst case scenario
(the)worst of it is that, complaining of changes
Wound up, tense
Wrap up! Be quiet!
Write something off, lost or no value
Writing on the wall, message of doom

### (3) Neutral Ground

Vexed question, one that is much discussed
(by) virtue of, because of
Vital statistics, of female waist, chest and hip sizes

(on the) wagon, abstention from alcoholic drinks
Wake up to, suddenly become aware of
Walk of life, calling or way of living
Walls have ears, not safe to talk here
Warts and all, including faults & disadvantages
Watch one's step, take care in all respects
(on the same)wavelength, same mind & opinion
(by) way of, for the purpose of doing
Wear several hats, hold more than one position
Wear the trousers, female rule in the home
Weigh up, calculate the prospects
What about …?  Will you consider this or that?
What's the odds?  What difference does it make?
When it comes to it, in reality
Whys and wherefores, the essential questions
(clip someone's) wings, reduce another's power
*Wiser after the event, saying*
Wish someone would *do* something, plea for help
(I'm)with you, I get your meaning
Words fail me, I cannot describe my feelings
(under wraps, secret for the time being
Wrap something up, conclude the matter

(spin a) yarn, long, probably unreliable story
You never can tell, it might or might not happen

Zero hour, the time an event is fixed to begin
Zero in on, get into focus

### 3) WHAT'S IN A NAME?

### 3.1) Memory test, What name did you say?

All but the name
        I remember everything else

Adam re-quoted
        I wouldn't know him from Adam!

Go by the face
        I never forget a face

Who's that person? - put me out of my misery!

### 3.2) Tell me who it is

I've got it now
        or I think I have

'You don't remember me, do you?'
        I don't care for a challenge like that; people shouldn't
        do it; it's embarrassing!

### 3.3) More to a name

Have to one's name
>   possessions, achievements

Name calling
>   derogatory remarks

Name-dropping
>   try to impress by assuming familiarity with the well-known

Name of the game
>   the important factor, the purpose

Namely
>   that is to say

Namesake
>   someone having the same name as oneself

Name the day
>   the date for the occasion

Put one's name down
>   apply for a job, declare an interest, sign a petition

Take a name in vain
>   belittle or use profanely

'Who shall be nameless'
>   people probably know already, or else it's too boring to have to repeat it

Namesake
>   someone with the same name

Name the day
  state date of the particular occasion

No names, no pack-drill
  if names are mentioned, someone will be punished

Take a name in vain
  belittle or use profanely

## 4) PERSONALITIES

**Names that go on and on.
Know your Man or your Woman.**

### 4.1) The Jacks and the Johnnies

All-right, Jack
> he is the one who is doing all right even when plenty are not and doesn't lose a moment to tell you so 'all work and no play makes Jack a dull boy.' Of course, Jack may not be his real name, but he is obvious enough.

Cheapjack
> dealer who continues to lower his price until he gets a sale

Every man Jack`
> everybody

Jack-in-office
> self-important, low ranking official

Jack-in-the-box
>he is  a toy who springs up when one opens the lid,
>but there are real people like him.

Jack Jones
>'on my Jack Jones' is to be alone

Jack on board
>so far as he is concerned, the ship may now sail and
>never mind the rest

Jack of all trades *('and master of none!')*
>the man who claims he can do every job under the sun

Jack Robinson
>*'Before you can say Jack Robinson'* remains a well-known
>phrase, the original with a reputation for being so fast
>when making a call that he was gone before he could be
>introduced.

Jack Tar
>the sailor with tar on his ropes and, one imagines, on
>his clothes as well .

Play the Jack`
>Play the rogue


**Try for 'Johnny'?**

John Bull
>large, stout-hearted emblem of he British nation if rather
>too portly to enter battle or fit a uniform

John Collins
> one presumes that the long gin-based drink John Collins
> was named after its creator

Johnny-cum-lately
> he has little experience, only a high opinion of himself

Johnny-head-in-air
> perhaps we should stand aside to allow him to pass
> and, hopefully, not return

Johnny's raw
> a beginner

## 4.2) Joes and Jimmies

Joe Bloggs is anyone at all,
Joe Soap not a person but a dirty, unpleasant task, and
Holy Joe religious and a zealot.

## Jimmies

Jimmy
> in the British navy there"s Jimmy-the-One, the senior
> lieutenant but usually with a rank above. Apart from
> him Dismal Jimmy is a confirmed pessimist.

### 4.3) Tom, Dick and Harry, together or separate

Tom, Dick and Harry, meaning – if not half the world, or everybody – the crowd that would invade your garden if given half a chance , so you don't wish to know them even though, individually, they might be charming., like

### Toms

Among Toms to be picked out for special attention one might mention:-

Doubting Thomas, the original being the follower of Jesus who didn't identify his Master until he saw the wounds; hence all sceptics by whatever name. *St John 20, 24-29)*

Tommy Atkins, and other Toms
Tommy Atkins is a private soldier of the British army as from the 19th century when a  recruiting form showing name, date and age gave *Tommy Atkins* as a specimen example.

Tom Bowling, buried at sea and one might not have heard of him but for being included as the touching epitaph in Sir

Henry Wood's ' selection of sea songs at the  'Last Night of the Proms' until quite recently.

Tomfool , tomfoolery (a fool and his tricks)

Tommy gun, a short-barrelled sub-machine gun

Tomahawk, a North American Indian war-axe

Tomboy, a romping girl

Tommyrot, nonsense

Tom Thumb, a dwarf, from an early children's story

Tommy shop, where  one purchased with vouchers

Tom Tiddler, character in a children's story who had a hard time trying to protect his gold

Tom-tiler (*or tyler)* a hen-pecked husband

Peeping Tom, one who spies on others

Uncle Tom, leading character in the popular American novel, *Uncle Tom's Cabin*

Of Dick and Harry we have mixed news.  There is Spotted Dick', a delicious currant sponge pudding,  Clever Dick, the know-all,  Dick Turpin, the 18th century highwayman, and Dick  Whittington, Lord Mayor of London in both fact and fiction in the 14th and 15th centuries.

As for Harry, 'Old Harry' is the devil , Bell Harry, the 15th century central tower of Canterbury Cathedral, and Harry used as a prefix :- for example, 'Harry-westers' for the town of

Haverfordwest in South Wales.

Nearer the present day 'Flash Harry' was the title awarded to he dapper orchestral conductor Sir Malcolm Sargent who never appeared otherwise.

## 4.4)  Nell and Nellie

'Not on your Nellie', *not in any circumstance whatsoever* has little to do with persons but is derived from London 'Cockney' rhyming slang, so called … *not on your nellie duff,* that is to say ('not in your puff' (not in your life)

Don't Let Poor Nellie Starve

For a real Nell, Nell as short for Eleanor, look to Nell Gwyn, born into poverty, a flower-seller, popular actress at the Drury Lane theatre of London and lover of  King Charles 11. 'Don't let poor Nellie starve,' said the king to his brother James (James 11) on his death-bed.  Nor did he.

## 4.5)  Grand Old Men, Granny and Aunt

Gladstone and the Duke of York

The former the long-serving Victorian prime minister W.E.Gladstone, of whom the Queen thought rather less of than some.  She complained that he lectured her as though addressing a committee.  Of the latter, second son of George 111, it was alleged that his greatest feat was to march his ten thousand troops up a hill, then down again.

'Granny Smith (any relation?) is a sweet green apple introduced to New South Wales by one Maria Ann Smith, while an agony aunt is one who attempts to sort out personal problems of her newspaper or magazine readers who write to her.

## 4.6)  Choose your uncle

Old Uncle Tom Cobbleigh and All

Now there is a legend that will never die.  It appears that a number of Devon 'worthies' borrowed a horse to get them to Widdicombe Fair many years ago, the famous Devon sheep and pony fair held every September.  There were seven of them altogether, old Uncle Tom Cobbleigh  being the last to get on:-
'

*Tom Pearse, Tom Pearse, lend me your grey mare*
*All along, down along, out along lee,*
*For I want to go to Widdicombe Fair*
*With Bill Brewer, Jan Stewer, Peter Gurney, Peter Davey*
*Dan'l Whiddon, Harry Hawk, Old Uncle Tom Cobbleigh*
*and all,*
*Old Uncle Tom Cobbleigh and all.*

. . . . . . . . . . . . .

'Bob's your uncle'

For an uncle story with a difference, 'Bob's your uncle' is the appropriate expression when something apparently difficult is achieved without effort. 'Bob' being the nickname for a Robert, the original here to possess an uncle of this name  was the 19th century politician,  Briish member of Parliament A.J.Balfour, happily promoted by his uncle Robert, Lord Salisbury.

Have a 'Dutch uncle' and one is then at the mercy of a scolding senior relative.  Apparently, Dutch family discipline had a reputation for being strict if not severe. Have a sense of humour and your uncle Joe is none other than Joseph Stalin.

## 4.7) One meets all types

One meets all types that, together with the afore-mentioned, remain on exhibition, namely:-

Smart Alec, another clever chap, or thinks he is, from (originally) the American 1860's but with modern bumptious counterparts

Merry Andrew (still around if also by any other name. The original was said to be an eccentric court jester in the time of Henry V111

Big Bertha, long-range German gun of World War 1

Big brother.  Succumb!

Billy of 'like billy-o', meaning very fast.  The model was almost certainly an early steam locomotive of George Stephenson 'running like bill-y-o', although other claimants include Nino Biglio, swashbuckling servant of Garibaldi.
Black-eyed Susan, large daisy with yellow petals and black centre

Blue Peter  … he's a blue design on a flag of white squares

Busy Lizzie, a fast-growing house plant

…...............................................

Cunning Isaac, attributed to Isaac, only son of Abraham, and to Isaacs ever since; a difficult cross to bear

Darby and Joan  the long-lived happy couple who in all their life together never had a quarrel.  They go back to the *Gentleman's Magazine* of 1735, then celebrated in song

Dogberry, Shakespeare's officious policeman from *Much Ado about Nothing*, who is apparently still around

Dolly Varden, the floppy hat with the drooping brim of her original creator

Heath Robinson, inventor of intricate, totally fictitious machinery that might need a miracle to make it work

Hobson's choice means no choice, Hobson having a stable and horse-hire business in 18th century Cambridge and when the customer had to accept the first mount that was offered

Home, James of *'Home, James and don't spare the horses'* from the time when the wealthy had their own horse, carriage and driver to go with it. Probably rather a nice fellow, obliging type who 'knew where his bread was buttered' -what he had to do to oblige his employer.

Hoorah Henry, upper-class ne'er-do-well who can 'wreck a joint' just like his lower-rated equivalent

Jekyll and Hyde, twin characters from within a single person , from a novel by R. L Stevenson

Mickey Finn, a doped drink

Molly Coddle, any pampwered creature *mollycoddled*

Nobby Clark ... all Clarks are 'Nobbies'

Nosey Parker, who needs to know what you are doing, the first being no less a personage than Matthew Parker, Archbishop of Canterbury 1559-75, well noted for his frequent Articles of Enquiry

Old Sobersides, any serious old man

Paul Jones, naval hero of long ago, until acquiring additional fame as a popular 1920's dance

Proper Charlie, some poor ineffectual being who has proliferated alarmingly since his 19th century origins

Sally Army, the Salvation Army
Sally Lunn, a sweet tea-cake served with butter

Simon-pure, whatever is genuine (*from an 18th century French novel*)

Sweet Fanny Adams *( sweet f.a. In sailors' shorthand).*
With the original an unfortunate who met a tragic end, it is difficult to see how she came to embody the naval version with the meaning of 'nothing at all'.
Wally, a foolish person; also a familiar alternative for Walter

Walter Mitty, day-dreaming hero of writer James Thurber
.

## 4.8) Waltzing Matilda

who was never a lady but a bag of swag bounced along the ground and brought to fame by the Australian poet A.B. 'Banjo' Paterson ...

*Once a jolly swagman camped by a billabong*
*Under the shade of a coolibah tree,*
*And he sang as he watched and waited till his billy boiled -*
*You'll come a-waltzing Matilda with me*

## 5)    NAME THE PLACE

No doubt about it, places work on the mind, continually ferment and never leave one alone.   They take one back to childhood, quaint places very often with perhaps little significance for others. They remain, weave their magic and perhaps tempt one to return to them, take a fresh look.   But would that fresh look recapture the early experience? Not if the essential characters have been replaced by others that serve only to confuse the memory.

There are national magnets, too, if with the drawback for the modern eye of having lost the essential context, like, for example, the railway carriage where a world war cease-fire was signed.   Around our towns grand generals still ride their horses to victory if, sadly, to be ignored for being only statues. 'Nelson' looks down from Trafalgar Square.   But give me the little spot on the seafront at Cowes where I watched ocean liners crossing the Solent and knew all their tonnages.

*Buckets and spades were a bit tame after that.*

I never revisited, though   I'll admit to being tempted. What can never be physically regained are the tentacles of seemingly ordinary places that gripped one accidentally to remain a dominant part of one's life.

## 5.1) A place for everything, and everything in its place

A place can mean so many different things – from a place to live, to one's position in a queue, to the way furniture is arranged, to what is considered right or wrong, to where one sits at a table, on and on. But for most it's the domestic scene
that takes *pride of place* .

All over the place
     People have different ways of arranging furniture. Those with 'a tidy mind' will not tolerate what they consider to be a 'slapdash' (careless) arrangement where there is no proper order order and little to distinguish between articles and rubbish scattered everywhere, even up the staircase. Nothing ever gets put away. The same the next time..
     As for the kitchen there may be evidence of the night before, a crowded sink, but , of course, it is a free country!

     A bit of a squeeze!  (So much to get in)

     As homes become smaller because of the shortage of land and high  building costs, cupboard and shelf space become increasingly important.  For every two things there might be space for one only, and  *two into one won't go.* To keep month after month things that one is not currently using but what might 'come in handy' sometime is becoming a luxury of the past.
     On holiday one is again encouraged to be tidy. Campers should look as though they are enjoying life, not having an almighty struggle.  One can have separate 'rooms' even in a tent with, once again, a place for everything.

**5.2) A place in the sun or 'digs' in the home of another ? Or, if neither of these, what else?**

Did you find a place?

But it's *a far cry* (a big jump)from looking for a place to live or stay for any length of time.   For a start, how about 'digs' ('diggings'), temporary accommodation with or without meals in the home of another?  Other than that the hunt may be for a furnished apartment that one can share with a friend.

'Home is where you make it.'
Home must always *take first place.*

## 5.3) 'Places and places'

There are, of course,' places and places',  meaning to say that some are either better than others or better managed, even if they happen to be similarly listed in any advertisement and within a similar price-range.

Dreadful place

Most will exaggerate when it comes to describing a' dreadful place'.  It's human nature.   One or two things wrong from the start and you don't forgive the town, village, property or the long *traipse* (journey, walk, etc) just to get there.  Start right, however, and build up in the mind your image of *a smashing place ,* one that you would highly recommend and, likely as not, the image will remain, even grow.   First impressions count, but in a matter as  important as choosing a home,*give them the once-over,*check that they are correct.  And, of course, *one man's meat is another man's poison.* We don't all like the same thing
    What is annoying is meeting the person who thinks his is the only opinion worth considering and that you are a fool if you disagree or fail to take his advice.  The world being made as it is, there is always a place for him as well.

## 5.4)  Early Place

queue

The sooner the better, *first come, first served.* The trouble with this particular brand of philosophy is that the excitement of the chase leaves little time for thought. Gain or lose may be a matter of minutes, even seconds.

That said, there may be scope for a slow approach with something good on offer for any prepared to wait in a queue. It could be for hours, you might even need a sleeping bag; just hope that what you get as a  reward for your patience is what you wanted all along. Or lose a few places by checking first. It might be for a concert, and you still needed to pay.


There is nothing more welcome than the day when, after a period of doubts and stresses, everything *'falls into place.*

### 5.5) Find the right place

Short of time and unable to find the right place? It happens to all of us. It's maddening when street numbers go up alleys, having started in regular fashion along a highway. Lose your place. Most certainly!

But the worst place for losing your place *(if I may put it like that)* is at an airport, most especially a modern one that has cost billions. At the new Hong Kong example, the passenger transferring will first need to catch a train, then a series of lifts leading to arrowed escalators, then to a choice of departure zones, only to be redirected on reaching what *was* the right one.

Say no more!

### 5.6) Fall into place

Arrangements fall into place when one takes on some job or other commitment in which, at first, it is difficult to see one's way.

## 5.7) Funny kind of place

Judgements are mostly very individual in their conception so that any other person's ideas may strike one as queer – eccentric, funny.. .

'Funny, peculiar, and 'funny, ha-ha!'
    Distinguish whichever meaning from the context of what is being said.


## 5.8)  Great place

Call anything 'great' and you are passing a compliment, no doubt about that.
'Did you enjoy the drama?' …
'Great'.
'How's the job going?'
'Great'
Your wife like it here?'
'Great'.
You might be forgiven for wishing there were no such word any more in the English language, but 'you'd have a job', meaning to say it wouldn't be easy to get rid of it.  The chances are that if you are in England there will be place-names all around beginning with the word 'Great...' as well as some more modest ones starting with 'Little …'

    The choice is yours if you are 'going places' that is to say, making a good career and/or travelling..

## 5.9) Her own place

In the years since World War 11 there has been a positive revolution in the way that families house themselves. Soon after leaving school and getting their first job sons have opted for independence and, more recently, a girl, particularly if in business, nursing or one of the professions. She will want or demand 'her own place' even if it a shared place with a friend.

That apart, family units appear willing to shrink when the time comes and no longer expect a daughter or son to stop at home until marriage. Nor in Britain, unlike some other countries, is there any desire to nurture parents or any elderly relatives at all, and on the female side a grandmother may take pride in having 'her own place' given a spot of assistance to go with it – regular visits from a dutiful daughter should there be one handy with a spot of free time ... or the appearance of it. Sons are excused – *not their place.*

Great! Brilliant!

## 5.10) 'Have you a place for ?'

It's always good to be given something one needs or a gift of some desirable product one wouldn't buy for oneself. Or even that sudden unexpected thing one *didn't* want seeing that 'it's the thought that counts.'

So be prepared any time for a *'Have you got room for this?'* And hopefully remember who gave it lest it be offered back to the same person at a later date.


All over the place
    chaotic

Fall into place
    be resolved

Give a place the once-over
    make an inspection

Give place to
    be succeeded by

Go places
    be successful; travel

In place
    in the right place

Keep (or put) a person in his place
    humble

Lose one's place
    falter when reading a text

Out of place
        inappropriate, in the wrong place

Place in the sun
        an easy and pleasant place to live

Places and places
        some are better than others

(the) place to go to
        the place for a particular purpose

Pride of place
        in a prominent position

Put yourself in another's place
        imagine yourself in his position

Take first place
        be given precedence

Take one's place
        take one's proper position

Take the place of
        replace, substitute

Take to or against a place
        like or dislike a place

Take place
        occur, come to pass

Also available through Amazon

By the same author:-

Poems of North Cornwall

Was It Really Me?
( Childhood memoir )

Passport to Cornwall
( Search for a dream-house with the help of a dog and a caravan )

English Idiom 1      Roses all the Way

English Idiom 2      Speak From the Body

English Idiom 3      Look Up, Look Back